STOP OVERTHINKING

Brain hacks: rewire your brain for controlling your thoughts and feeling better.

Simple strategies for beginners, for getting better results in both business and life!

EDWARD BOLD

I'd like to dedicate this book to all those who have not yet developed the necessary attention for realizing that they are not living their lives, as they are just letting it slip while reliving their past and imagining their future

INDEX

CREDITS

I shall thank the stranger who inspired me into writing this book, when during a walk in the mountains, we found ourselves strangely agreeing on what it meant to "improve our thinking"

WARNING

The content of this book cannot be considered in any way as therapeutic advice as the author holds no legally valid title to suggest therapies.

The author therefore declines all responsibility for the self-managed use of the scientific information that is contained in this text and, by law, must invite you to consult your doctor before taking any action resulting from reading this book.

INTRODUCTION

That part of the path was particularly steep, and those who had traced it realized it, to the point of deciding to set up a sort of small refreshment area on the hill above. I still could not know from where I was, but a few minutes later I would have been able to take a break, sitting comfortably on a pair of trunks arranged horizontally and shaped like benches.

I was surprised to find someone else already there. I had no reason to feel that way, but the fact of not meeting anyone until that point had naively made me believe that I was the only one walking in that valley.

"I didn't think someone would hit the road before me" I said, trying to establish a courtesy dialogue.

"It was dark" I managed to hear, as by then I was already next to him.

His whispered answer made me think I had bothered him, so I silently repented about my approach.

I opened the backpack looking for water bottle and chocolate bar. I watched myself in my gestures, almost as if my embarrassment had forced me to measure anything I was ever going to say or do.

I endured that situation for a couple of excruciatingly long minutes, then I got up to walk, without having decided on whether to say "bye" or not.

"I must be sick, I just can't enjoy the beauty of this nature. I just keep on thinking about my past and imagining my future, again and again".

"I think it happens to everyone" I replied, without him having asked me anything.

IMPROVING THE THINKING

Better than many others, Buddhists have noticed how the human brain has an attitude which we can also observe in monkeys: like the animal we see jumping from one branch to another, our mind quickly passes from thought to thought, reliving past experiences with the memory and anticipating potential futures with our fantasy. Furthermore, we tend to pessimistically revise experiences which we consider negative, rather than imagining the worst scenarios for our future.

Obviously, nature wants us to review our mistakes in order for us to study more appropriate behaviors for the future, but also for preparing ourselves for the worst, allowing us to work out the best strategies to face such cases, too.

Thus, all of this will also prove extremely useful in terms of survival, but unlike other animals, man realizes that "thinking too much hurts". Above all, it hurts to think at the mercy of one's own mind, without being able to choose what to think.

This is over-thinking: it is literally defined as "thinking too much", technically it is more like "uncontrolled thinking", which precisely for this reason, is rather harmful.

It is therefore implied that one of the most immediate things we can do for our own personal well-being is "to improve our thinking", adopting strategies for preventing thoughts from bouncing back and forth, outside our control.

In the first part of this self-help text, these strategies are laid out conceptually, only to be successively revisited in the second part, through a list which incites to put them into practice, addressing the reader in first person.

PART 1

Even Shakespeare, in Romeo and Juliet, once wrote "teach me to forget about thinking", but it seems that the over-thinking problem is particularly present in our modern society, to the point that Susan Nolen-Hoeksema, head of the Department of Psychology at Yale University, states: "The world is suffering from an epidemic excess of thought".

However, the problem is indeed not just "thinking too much". As was said before, it is actually more the "useless thinking". In fact, again citing the researcher, over-thinking is "the tendency to respond to a discomfort by focusing on the causes and consequences of one's problems, without undertaking any concrete problem-solving action".

This explains why the problem is mostly feminine: women face emotional life and daily hardships with a perspective which is less oriented towards active problem-solving, which instead remains a peculiarly male feature.

Nonetheless, all interviewees, regardless of their gender, recognize that they think continuously and repetitively about the same topics, mainly work and family, thus manifesting all those attitudes which are telling of an unbalanced mental pattern: trouble concentrating, stress, not being at ease in silence, need to keep the radio or TV on in the background and compulsive checking of the smartphone.

Refining how the brain functions, facilitating new ways of thinking and reacting to the surrounding environment, can significantly improve the quality of life, and reducing instances when we're "thinking too much" is the first thing to pay attention to, when moving towards this direction.

THE CAUSES OF "THINKING TOO MUCH"

It is estimated that each and every one of us produces in between 50,000-60,000 thoughts every day, but first we should ask ourselves which ones are useful, which ones are necessary and, ultimately, even which ones are true.

Indeed, we have to in fact distinguish between constructive thinking, aimed at better living the environment we live in, and mental rumination, which according to psychologist Roberta Cassuti, is "a way of thinking based on the negative evaluation of oneself and past episodes of his life, which prevents him from having active and healthy behaviors, and consequently, from finding a solution to the occurrence of a real problem".

Self-reflection can in fact have a constructive function, however it often happens to only establish an uncomfortable situation, because the thinking pattern is exclusively focused on causes and effects, without any practical use.

The moments in which it is easier to fall victim to over-thinking are in fact precisely those during which we are not solicited to seek solutions for a problem, such as when we are driving, or in the shower, or maybe drying our hair.

But why, precisely, do we end up swept away by the waters of this uncontrolled river of thoughts, seemingly impossible to contain?

We think too much because we lack overview, and are confused by details. So we end up repeating a continuous analysis of the worst possible scenario, because we perceive ourselves as in danger.

This makes us understand how over-thinking is a scourge of the modern age, linked to the insecurity and confusion that the same society has created, bombarding single individuals with information and preconceived schemes which are characteristic of negative journalistic sensationalism.

In all likelihood, the medieval man was much more anchored to his everyday life, and his head was not lost behind his thoughts.

IT'S ALL NORMAL

Although modern life has certainly made over-thinking more frequent, it must be clearly specified that it is an absolutely normal phenomenon, since it is a simple consequence of how the human mind works.

Our good old shoemaker from the early Middle Ages was always intent on sewing the shoes of some noble knight, and often brooded on what he had done the day before, or was worried about tomorrow, but simply put, the news didn't keep on bothering him about apocalyptic world economy scenarios. His world was only as big as the village he lived in, and his worries were limited accordingly.

We said that it is normal for the human mind to develop associative thoughts, because association is how thinking proceeds, but the peculiar state of confusion of "thinking too much" is a consequence of the fact that one is not sufficiently centered and mentally organized.

We are not trying to recover from an illness, but to find a greater inner balance.

Technically, we must observe that we are faced with a degeneration in analytical thought and problem-solving-based attitude, which men are more inclined to than women, which is why the latter are more subject to it: they're less anchored to resolve, they fantasize more easily and end up worrying about the future.

Furthermore, the researchers noted that the problem manifests itself especially among perfectionists, who are inevitably inclined towards wondering on how they could have improved what they did, and how they should behave in the best possible way for the future.

Even the depressed and those with little memory seem to be more likely to lose themselves in their thoughts. This is what researchers at Collage University in London suggest, as they also observed a greater number of pre-frontal cortex cells in these subjects. This physiological feature, as much as it should facilitate them in analytical thinking, seems to also have the degeneration of the same as a potential consequence.

From the view of traditional Chinese medicine, this phenomenon is instead attributed to individuals with material and spiritual features, which show a prevalence of the earth element, due to their spontaneous predominance in activities related to the energy complex of stomach, spleen and pancreas: when these organs are not in the right balance, they trigger anxiety, worry and unbridled thought activity.

NEFARIOUS CONSEQUENCES

Although in the previous chapter it was highlighted how over-thinking is an absolutely normal phenomenon, in how the human being's way of thinking is structured, it doesn't take away the fact that it is an attitude with quite the nefarious consequences on life quality.

In fact, it happens that the slightest cue drags us into a spiral of negative thoughts, which eventually ends up stealing away our joy and enthusiasm.

Indeed, we must recognize that it is a problem in itself: we lose our lives, thinking about life itself!

First of all, we "lose" our life because we don't pay attention to it, and without doing so, life is not lived: you're definitely not taking a walk in a forest if you don't enjoy anything about nature all around, because you're thinking about that speech you're going to have with your company next day, rather than how you will dress for the occasion. The unconscious probably also benefits from all of the environment's sensory stimuli, but not realizing it inevitably makes you lose much of the experience.

And with the premise that "thinking too much" mainly revolves around potential negative scenarios, it is easy to imagine how it can deprive us of some possible futures, which could for example become reality when meeting new people, and be the cause of anxiety, panic attacks, depression and irritability.

Consequently, due to the depressive state, use of alcohol and drugs in general should not be surprising.

CHAPTER 1

THE POWER OF PERSONALITY

Developing a well-structured personality is a key element in reducing over-thinking.

In fact, living in peace with oneself helps to limit this depleting mental attitude, very much common to everyone. Let's see how to actively intervene on the different facets of our personality.

ACCEPTING OVER-THINKING AND YOURSELF

It must be accepted very serenely that this problem not only exists, but is common to all mankind.

It is an attitude linked to the desire to have control over everything, which can be overcome by accepting the possibility of making mistakes and that life is not perfect as one would like.

It might be useful to develop awareness, confirmed by experience, that by brooding over things will not be resolved, but will keep getting worse.

It has also proved effective to not just accept what is outside, but also to turn your attention to you and your emotions, forgiving yourself for your mistakes. This sort of absolution for what you committed previously indeed avoids to continually relive the film of a past, for which you may feel as the guilty protagonist. Nonetheless, it is necessary to develop a mental state which places forgiveness towards oneself together with gratitude towards others, as these two feelings are capable to completely overturn the exhausting spiral in which we end up so easily.

DOMINATING EMOTIONS

We all tend to suffer from the emotions we feel, tending to identify them with ourselves.

A good technique to get away from our emotions is to ask ourselves why are we feeling them, and try to write it down: re-reading on the sheet, we will somehow be "observers" of what overwhelmed us before.

TAKING RESPONSIBILITY

Feeling responsible and in control of any situation is the most effective way to get out of it at will.

Believing in common facts, such as "the economy is bad" or "people don't like me", means instead to put oneself in the position of the one to whom things "happen", and therefore doesn't have the possibility to create anything.

A person who chooses to be responsible approaches the events of life by smugly saying to himself: "I made this thing happen to me, I will surely need it and I can still change it when I want!".

PROMOTING SELF-ESTEEM

Obviously, a great personality is endowed with a strong self-esteem, and knows the value of developing it over time, gratifying himself with the successes he achieves over the course of his life.

A person with these features will make plans for his future in a healthy way, without falling prey to the endless occurrence of "thinking too much".

In fact, perhaps exaggerating a little, he will feel indestructible and ready to face anything.

BEING POSITIVE

A proverb explains that we don't learn from what happened to us, but from how we have been able to react to what happened to us.

It is precisely our reaction that highlights the difference between positive thinking and actually being positive: the faith with which we react to the event makes the difference between putting ourselves definitively at peace with what we have lived, and instead preparing and reliving it in our heads a thousand times!

BEING GOOD TO OURSELVES

Experiencing one's own existence also means pampering yourself and always keeping an eye on things. Like any other well-established habit, the propensity to "think too much" is not easy to overcome, and to treat yourself kindly while working on it is definitely crucial.

CHAPTER 2

THE POWER OF RATIONALITY

The human being is the only animal species to which reasoning has been acknowledge, and for this reason, intelligence is considered a qualifying characteristic of a person's value.

We therefore see some useful techniques for rationally reducing over-thinking.

LOGICALLY FACING THE PROBLEM

There are two causes for which thoughts are magnified and echo in our heads: the human tendency to "have a problem" (and therefore worry about nonsense in case you have nothing more serious to pay attention to), and it is just as human to emotionally depend on other people's judgments.

Both must be dealt with reason.

Many times it is enough to just realize that you are looking at the small pile of earth made by a mole in your garden, as if it were a mountain, simply because you don't have any more serious problems. In fact, 95% of what we usually fear will never happen!

All of history's philosophers have noticed that man tends to create small personal dramas on his own, giving meaning to things which intrinsically have none.

We must always ask ourselves how much the thought that today we cannot get out of our heads will prove to be important in the long term, so as to be limited to what really matters.

It is also useful to repeat what was realized, starting the sentence with the words "The truth is that...", in order to resize the shadow to the real stature of who projected it.

As for the judgment of others, reason teaches us to relax, because others are almost never thinking of us, but will most likely be mulling over their own problems.

Indeed, the invitation of logic is to base one's thoughts exclusively on facts and not on assumptions.

BISECTING THE PROBLEM

Much of the confusion you want to eliminate when you decide to improve your way of thinking, comes from the fact that you perceive the problem as a whole, and this does not allow you to face it.

The invitation is therefore to mentally breaking down what you're thinking of into pieces, so that these parts can be addressed individually and in sequence, with the daily commitment to assess the progress of your work.

It must be specified that the individual pieces are not the problem's details, because it is precisely over these that one gets lost when "thinking too much"! Otherwise, a correct procedure in this "bisection" could be to start off by asking yourself what is the purpose of the recurring thought, and then what are the consequences of thinking that way, and finally, what are the actions that thought pushes into doing.

As a last note, it has to be specified to avoid embarking on this speculative analysis in the late afternoon or evening, because the peculiar mental fatigue of that hour of the day would not allow to achieve the desired results.

SEARCHING FOR THE TRIGGERING ELEMENT

Another very useful approach to overcoming over-thinking is to look for its trigger.

Very often, in fact, the mental chatter originates for something that is often before our eyes, as for example a pile of unfilled mail could be.

It is therefore important to observe if something in the environment we live in periodically presents an opportunity to trigger the problem, and take action to remove this cause.

TELLING YOU WHAT YOU THINK

Even telling yourself aloud your own recurring thoughts offers the opportunity to ridicule them in the eyes of your own rationality: it is very easy for them to appear significantly smaller, compared to what they seem when echoing over within the head.

CHAPTER 3

THE POWER OF ACTION

In this chapter we will discuss how to facilitate success in overcoming over-thinking, by means of some virtuous lifestyle changes.

Particularly, the effectiveness of creating new habits, especially related to action, is demonstrated in both physical activity and nutrition.

CREATING NEW HABITS

In order to avoid being the victim of uncontrolled thoughts, it is useful to gain control of one's thoughts through voluntary establishment of new habits.

It is a way of remodeling one's mind through two different categories of habits: those designed to develop practical mechanisms which make life simpler, and those aimed at enjoying the present moment.

An example of the first category is to agree with all members of the family on where to put the car keys after having used it: taking the habit of hanging them on a hook, maybe placed behind the entrance door, is a functional procedure which frees a small part of everyone's mind.

Differently enough, the second category involves all those new habits which can be established with the sole purpose of appreciating life in its development. These are things which might seem unnecessary, like remembering to watch the sunset every evening or, paying attention to the taste and consistency of food in the act of chewing, but will prove very useful for freeing the mind.

REPLACING THINKING WITH DOING

If over-thinking is neither creative nor fun, there's no reason to linger.

Instead, it must be immediately replaced with action: doing things, rather than thinking and rethinking details.

That's what Nike suggests when we read its slogan "Just do it": action in itself contains the momentum needed to unlock thought.

This is not surprising, since it is a simple consequence of the fact that it was just too much thinking that used to block action.

EXERCISING

Movement of one's body is the action which most directly affects one's mood and thinking, and therefore, special attention must be given to it.

That is because the endorphins produced during physical activity create euphoria, by slowing down over-thinking, and because the stressful situation the body is subjected to during sport removes attention from thinking: if we're out of breath, it will be difficult to chase the thoughts in our heads!

Any body movement, even just playing or walking, defuses the spiral leading to depression, and in particular, everything which significantly involves breathing is a true antidote to uncontrolled thinking.

EATING WELL

Even adopting a healthy diet leads to extraordinary results in terms of mental lucidity.

In general, it would be better to prefer raw or at least not too processed food, because it is more easily digestible.

In fact, the intestinal transit of food significantly influences our thinking, because the microbiome, the bacterial flora inhabiting it and developing as a result of the foods we eat, determines what we think and desire.

This is the reason why we often refer to the intestine as a second brain: we could say that the microorganisms we host "think for us", without us realizing it.

Even drinking a lot of water facilitates digestion, because it dilutes the toxicity of what we ate, and is therefore an excellent antidote to "thinking too much", like the consumption of a large quantity of fresh fruit and vegetables, which are very moisturizing and equally rich in phytonutrients, which stimulate good mood.

CHAPTER 4

THE POWER OF INNER PEACE

Over-thinking is a new name for something that man has known since ancient times, and has always faced with different practices.

COMING BACK TO THE PRESENT

When you "think too much", you move away from the present moment in the direction of past or future events, usually developing negative thoughts and concerns.

Everything revolves around the question "what if...?", and the subsequent interminable past and future analysis.

This attitude is easily understood, by remembering that the human brain works by associations, and that the latter are biologically represented by neural connections: as the individual grows, the number of those connections increases, developing an inevitable predisposition to associative thinking and consequent over-thinking.

"Returning to the present "is therefore a practice to be consciously implemented, through conscious attention, because the human brain naturally tends to move away from the moment it is currently living.

You can do this by anchoring your focus onto the details of the environment you are interacting with, and forcing yourself to stay there, at least until a habit has developed for this too.

PRACTICING MEDITATION OR YOGA

All the many meditative practices have as their first objective this attention to the present that we want to develop, and offer specific techniques for reaching this goal.

There are many, but they all teach us to clear the mind: you won't need to assume the Lotus Position or to pray to Buddha, but to momentarily give up all of that daily life which keeps us in the whirlwind of thinking.

Many times it is enough to create a dedicated space to go regularly at a specific time, for entering into a state of mind which is favorable for concentration, and forget the thoughts of every day.

There are even more specific techniques for facilitating the achievement of this goal, perhaps by fixing the hypnotic flame of a candle, but in any case, consider it will take time to become familiar before enjoying the fruits of your commitment.

Eckhart Tolle stands out among the audience's favorite authors on the subject of meditation, and among techniques, particularly popular are those requiring to close your eyes, and pay attention to the breath and bodily sensations of your muscles.

Yoga then combines the advantages of meditation and a sort of almost static postural gymnastics, able to interact deeply with the mechanisms of thought, giving extraordinary benefits already after the first hours of class. Not everyone will feel prone to yoga, but it is definitely worth a try.

GIVING YOURSELF UP TO GOD

Reclining mentally in the assumption that God is pleased with the attitudes of all his children, made in his image and likeness, is a form of abandonment which guarantees the tranquility necessary for avoiding falling victim to continuous and uncontrolled thinking.

This attitude is extremely functional, because it releases that desire for control over the world, which is at the basis of over-thinking.

CHAPTER 5

USEFUL STRATEGIES

In this chapter we will describe some strategies which were recognized as useful for managing the uncontrolled succession of thoughts in the mind, and to be able to lead a more balanced life accordingly.

They are simple techniques which can reach a goal, that will also be able to reduce daily stress levels.

Ultimately, they teach how to manage anxiety by recognizing what triggers it, staying in the present, focusing on what you are doing, and doing yoga, rather than just assuming a posture showing greater self-confidence.

These are suggestions which have proved useful to a large number of people, listed so that the reader can experience them to discover those most in tune with his way of being. For some people, instead, it might prove even more effective to learn to laugh and smile more often, rather than simply get rid of boring daily activities, learning to delegate them to others.

BEING ALTRUISTS

Since over-thinking is originated by an extremely focused thought, it is useful to shift your attention to something as far as possible from the analytical and calculating thinking which characterizes it.

In this sense, focusing on making other people happy is extraordinarily effective, because it frees us from the dynamics which trigger, but above all maintain, the continuous rumination of thoughts in search of that "something more" which often coincides with one's own interest.

CREATING FALSE MEMORIES

When we find ourselves entangled in obsessively thinking about the past, most times we'll mentally trace those experiences which were not as we would have liked.

Since something is though specifically because it

didn't go as expected, or because you are not happy with the way things went, a good idea is to "change the past", meaning to create a false memory instead of the real one.

If a job interview went wrong because you were not able to meet the interlocutor's expectations with your answers, you can mentally relive the experience by imagining it was a success, and refused that job for a personal choice: tracing a memory by modifying it to your liking offers the possibility to empty it of its negativity, to the point of no longer being target of an insistent thought.

WRITING YOUR RECURRENT THOUGHTS

Writing thoughts coming back with insistence is a way to get rid of them because it allows you to observe it critically, as it will create distance between you and the thought itself: it is no longer in the head, but on a sheet out there!

A reality and circumscribed consistency has been given to what was an indefinite thought, but above all it has been placed where it will no longer tend to associate itself with anything.

The strategy is very simple: we need to write the

recurring thought with the only care of describing it with the darkest shades, in order to get the worst possible scenario out of the head. Any other thought related to the same situation will have no reason to worry, precisely because it will seem nothing compared to it.

This technique can also be transformed into a daily appointment dedicated to mental health: every evening, at a pre-established time, you will make a commitment to write a diary of the day's events, complete with all the sensory data received, as well as your future goals. This exercise reciprocates the commitment it requires with greater attention to the flow of your life, which immediately translates into an increase in mental lucidity, and ultimately, reduced propensity into over-thinking.

MIND MAPPING

Another strategy for distancing yourself from what you always have in your head consists in reproducing, always on paper, the mental map of your thoughts, in an exactly associative manner as it takes shape.

On paper, every thought is represented by a circle,

with a few words describing it. You will start with the first recurring thought that comes to mind, and place it at the center of the sheet, then connect it to other circles containing thoughts arising immediately by free association. And so on.

After a while, you will find yourself with a drawing, made up of several circles containing words and linked together, which represent everything you confusedly thought of. It also seems that using different colors for different circles also slows the flow of ideas in a beneficial way.

Ultimately, the final sheet reflects the thought, but above all the way of thinking, of the person who designed it, and hanging it on a wall and observing it while walking in the room is an excellent idea to further distance yourself from what was bothering you: the results achievable with something so simple are incredible!

THE EMPTY CHAIR TECHNIQUE

In over-thinking we need to assess two distinct problems: we believe we are our thoughts, and we believe that our thoughts represent reality. Neither of these two statements is true.

In particular, thinking doesn't mean representing reality, it is rather an activity linked to its interpretation and organization, through the creation of categories aimed at action.

To "explain all this to ourselves", it would be useful to imagine yourself in an empty chair in front of you, and to talk by making an objective analysis of the situation as if we were addressing another person.

SEARCH FOR SUPPORT IN OTHERS

Those who "think too much" have the unhealthy habit of wanting to create at least 3 reserve plans for each situation.

Sometimes it is enough to ask a trusted person what he would do if he had that particular problem, to realize that everything is much simpler, and there is no need to mentally develop so many possible scenarios and face all potential developments.

This support can also be requested to a therapist, with the unquestionable advantage of relating to a person who has the necessary skills to best handle requests and doubts.

CHAPTER 6

CONCLUSIONS

Thinking qualifies the human being, but thinking too much and in a compulsive manner can seriously hinder our life quality, and prove to be something we need to face, in order to protect our own well-being in the long term.

Summing up in a few words, the invitation is to abandon preconceptions but above all mental schemes, in order to be able to love who you are, what you do and the extraordinary ability to improve ourselves; but above all, to love the same precise desire to take an active path in this direction.

PART 2

This second part of the book lists some useful daily strategies to stop "thinking too much".

The reader is addressed directly with the intention of snapping him away from a situation he recognizes only partially, as he is rooted in his way of being and with which he identifies his personality.

The text is structured in short chapters dealing with individual issues, for allowing to compare them by returning to the individual passages and insisting on them as needed.

ADMITTING TO HAVING A PROBLEM

The first step towards healing is always the one during which you recognize the existence of the disease. It is a sort of diagnosis, without which you will not be able to begin your journey. In the case of over-thinking, it is essential that you admit the mental confusion generated by your incessant brooding on the same problems, and recognize the fact that this has never led to their solution.

In particular, "thinking too much" is defined as the feeling of not being able to get out of the flow of thoughts which overwhelm you, to the point of feeling frustrated and unhappy.

Since you have surely discovered that these sensations disappear with the same rapidity and spontaneity with which they have presented themselves, you may be tempted to ignore them, while waiting to get better without undertaking any action. This is obviously a partial admission of the problem, because you are not really acknowledging it as such, in the hope of not having to face it.

In human logic, following the admission of having a debilitating problem, one needs to take some action to solve it, and this is what you are already doing by reading this book. You simply need to have the perseverance to persist, with determination.

YOU ACKNOWLEDGE YOU ARE NOT GUILTY

You have no fault of your continuous brooding, it is not a consequence of some kind of behavioral error or genetic defect: it is a "disease" that afflicts the whole of humanity, because the human brain is wired to think a lot, and in an associative manner.

Furthermore, the number of connections between your brain neurons increases with the passing of the years, and consequently worsens the tendency to associative thinking, and therefore over-thinking.

Susan Nolen-Hoeksema, an expert in this field, also specifies how your brain is set up to be able to think by working a mass of information where thoughts are intrinsically woven together with memories, not divided split into isolated compartments, and therefore a state of sad mood or a moment of bad temper are just what is needed to unleash a general branched negativity on the whole brain network, that makes you see everything black.

Your brain is designed to work this way, you're not guilty for this, but you don't have to give up improving your life quality.

GIVE UP CONTROL AND FORGIVE YOURSELF

If you are reading this book, you are probably a control freak, and you like to firmly hold the reins of your existence.

There is nothing wrong with your attitude, but this is not the case. This time you have to learn to surrender: life is not like you had expected, nor will you live what you had imagined. But there is nothing wrong with that, either.

The same ability of being surprised at life that thrilled you as a young man, has now given way to a greater need for security, mixed with then-unknown concerns, and it is this that has ultimately developed in you the need to keep everything under control.

Nobody demands you to give up an attitude which gives you peace of mind, but don't overdo it. Otherwise, you will end up easy victim of repetitive and uncontrollable thoughts in which you will manifest future catastrophic scenarios, without realizing that they have no real chance of being realized. And those same scenarios will require the study of an imaginary plane in reaction to the events, with all the details necessary to implement it. And then you will also find yourself thinking about another backup plan, in case the first one fails. And then new thoughts developed by association will follow each other... and you'll find yourself completely absorbed in over-thinking, while life flows before your eyes and you're unable to see it.

Is this clear? A reasonable need for security can explain your mental attitude; but it must not become a pretext to indulge in it, but rather a cue into forgiving yourself for having procrastinated the moment in which you have to face the problem until now.

SHOW YOURSELF HAPPY

Maybe you never thought about it, but you have the chance to control your thoughts.

The irrational fears which are peculiar of over-thinking hinder your personal evolution, but they can be avoided by "changing your way of thinking".

I state that it will not be easy for you to divert your thoughts on what makes you calm, when you are assailed by anguish and negativity. This happens because it is technically difficult to change individual thoughts, since they are under the control of the unconscious mind.

So I suggest instead that you commit yourself to "behaving like a happy person": act and show yourself happy, everything else will follow by itself.

Let me explain. The idea is that if you act as if you are happy, your unconscious will slowly notice this and start believing in it, changing your basic belief system, and over time, developing thoughts which are characteristic of happy people, and promoting actions that you usually see in such people.

It may seem unbelievable, but the beliefs underlying your behavior can be rewritten by forcing the attitudes that you would like to become yours: this suggestion is not a void deception towards yourself and others, but a valid tool for working on our subconscious.

Even just remembering to smile more often will make you believe at a deep level to be a happy person, and make you feel better, consequently stimulating better thoughts and gradually changing your basic mood: show yourself happy, and you will become happy!

STOP COMPLAINING

Your Ego really likes to complain: it does so by assuming the role of the eternal victim, of people and situations. This way, he can justify any of your attitudes as a result of "what they did to him or what happened to him".

Unfortunately, complaints attract so much negativity in your life; not for some obscure esoteric dynamic, but simply because they rewrite your belief system in the opposite direction to that promoted in the previous chapter.

You must strive to grasp the positivity of every event or situation, and you can do so by generically feeling grateful to the world for what you are or have. Feeling grateful every day and making it a sort of morning ritual is in fact an extraordinary opportunity to overcome the tendency to complain about the present, and regret past mistakes.

GIVE UP PERFECTIONISM

A tendency to perfectionism is a problem, because in the long term, it will make you see everything as extremely tiring, and you'll feel heavy because of that.

Undoubtedly, there are people which are more prone to perfectionism by their nature, but it is an attitude that always contributes to "thinking too much", because it promotes the incessant mental search for a better solution than the one already found: you put yourself in a situation of eternal confrontation, from which you'll perpetually emerge defeated.

It is not unlikely that the desire for perfection will become an obsessive and nagging thought for you, preventing you from enjoying what you are experiencing.

It is right for you to aim at excellence, but you must also know how to play serenely, because life is trial and error, and knowing how to accept your mistakes is crucial: only by not doing anything you won't do anything wrong!

DISTRACT YOURSELF

Is your mind going towards its usual thoughts? Route it elsewhere, treating her like a capricious child.

To distract yourself, it is enough to turn your attention to what you are doing, and it may be a good idea to take a little break for dedicating yourself to another activity: you don't have to "stop doing", rather try to "do something else".

The goal is just not being assailed by an uncontrolled cascade of thoughts, not avoiding to have them at all.

There's nothing wrong with looking at thoughts like birds flying over your head, you just have to stop them from nesting in your hair!

Another beautiful image to be inspired from was given to us by Deepak Chopra, who described thoughts as running clouds, inviting to concentrate only on the sky, always present beyond the clouds.

BE DIFFERENTLY CREATIVE

Some studies reveal that creatives are the most likely people to be victim of over-thinking, precisely because their mind has a propensity towards the activity of thinking in an associative manner.

If you are one of these people, it is useful to try to vent your creativity in a different way: less mental and more manual.

You will discover that you can satisfactorily express your creativity even through an artistic expression, which includes a manual aspect; for example, playing a musical instrument, modeling clay or painting, and you will also find that these activities make you feel better, just because they divert part of your energy into the physical world, instead of concentrating it all in your head.

BREAK OUT OF PATTERNS

The mental patterns and consequent obsessive thoughts you want to get rid of are placed in front of you by your everyday environments.

This is because known situations, images and sounds trigger association with past memories.

The solution is to amaze yourself by breaking out of both your mental and behavioral patterns: the mental patterns are the walls of your beliefs in which you have imprisoned the natural spontaneity of your mind, while behavioral patterns are the habits you repeat every day.

You will greatly benefit from behaving in a less rational way, every now and then: you may occasionally take the tram instead of the fastest subway, or rather go to lunch in the farthest restaurant.

Change has great value.

BREATHE PROPERLY

Oxygen is the most important nutrient for your body: you can stay several months without eating, a few days without drinking, but only a few seconds without breathing.

Breathing is, however, an activity as important as it is underestimated. In fact, since it is involuntary, few people actually worry about "breathing well".

In particular, shallow breathing involving only the upper part of the lungs without completely emptying them can be a consequence of the general state of depression, which is peculiar of those who "think too much": the pressure caused by thoughts puts a strain on even the most natural activities, such as breathing. Frustration causes the breath to become labored.

Furthermore, the opposite is also true: those who breathe badly aggravate their confusion, because they reduce the influx of oxygen to the brain.

The easiest way to unlock the situation is therefore to consciously seek deep breathing, waiting for it to become an involuntary habit again. Breathing will help you to ease the pressure and reconnect with Mother Earth.

A good breathing technique, able for bringing mind and body into a state of absolute relax, consists in lying down and then inspiring with the nose for about two seconds, then exhaling with the mouth, all for a minimum of 10 minutes.

This simple exercise will help you reduce carbon dioxide in the blood, with beneficial effects on the adrenal system and the obsessive nature of thinking.

Breath is life and, as such, it can also benefit on your mental state.

WALKING WITH YOUR HEAD HIGH

A peculiar posture unites all people perpetually afflicted by a dark blanket of recurring thoughts: eyes on the ground and shoulders slouched forward.

Willingly changing this postural attitude reflects on the emotional state that caused it.

An old story tells of a healer who advised to count the crows to heal from "bad thoughts": forced to look up in search of birds, his patients immediately felt better, without understanding why.

If this suggestion may seem silly to you, you must know that you are giving up a very useful tool for solving your problems.

PRACTICE SPORTS

Ancient Latins already were quoted saying "mens sana in corpore sano", recognizing that exercise is the best way to discharge anxiety and negativity.

Choose a sport that you like and makes you feel good, but above all, practice it frequently and regularly.

Physical activity stimulates the production of beneficial endorphins, and if you take the care of choosing an outdoor activity, you will also enjoy the advantages offered by sunlight: the latter has an antidepressant effect which improves mood, in addition to stimulating vitamin D production.

Practicing sports in nature also makes the activity even more beneficial, as you will be surrounded by a beauty that your unconscious will not fail to notice.

Moreover, if you dare to dedicate yourself to a new sport, you could discover qualities that you didn't even believe you had, and find yourself in a decidedly better context than the narrow starting situation, since besides a better body, you will have your mind occupied in the initial learning phase of gestures and logic of the sport activity you choose.

SPEAK LESS, WRITE MORE

Especially if you are a woman, you may be tempted to think that it is useful to "get it all out of your system", but actually, this is rarely beneficial.

In particular, talking about grievances with another person with a tendency to over-think will worsen the emotional situation of both people, since your negative thinking will influence your interlocutor and vice-versa, in un exhausting spiral.

The best way to take your problems to the outside is writing, because it allows you to put on paper everything that swirls in your head in a confused way: the sole action of writing brings clarity, because it forces you to mentally sort things, implicitly addressing them the moment they surface.

A written list helps you see things in black over white, and fully gain awareness of them.

CREATING ALTERNATIVES

The first flaw of those who think too much is that they tend to remain stuck on their point of view, and reinforce it by rethinking it repeatedly.

This approach is absolutely not aimed at solving problems, but only on thinking about them.

The most therapeutic thing you can do is writing a list of thoughts other than those you automatically process, forcing you to develop alternatives and neural pathways that you are not familiar, or usual to you.

Combine a different idea with the thoughts you usually nurture, ask yourself how you would deal with the situation in which you find yourself in an alternative way. It's about reinterpreting Apple's "Think differently" slogan, in light of your ability to create alternatives to your usual approach towards life: what would you think if you weren't you?

BE IN THE MOMENT

When you get lost behind your thoughts, you are in fact in your past or your future, but you are never in the present moment.

You must remember instead, that the here and the time are the only dimension on which you have power, and the only one you can use to change the course of your life. Living means thinking about the present.

Lau Tzu claimed that when you are depressed you are living in the past, and that when you are anxious you are in the future, whereas only when you are at peace are you in the present. With these words he emphasized the inclination of human beings into losing themselves behind the events of yesterday and tomorrow, forgetting that the only moment that can really be lived today is, indeed today, but also that this continuous protracting into the future or retreating towards the past inevitably makes you unhappy and negative.

Meditation can help you acquire the necessary awareness for living the present with serenity, focusing on the moment without judgment. It is about accepting and recognizing your thoughts and then letting them go, be they positive or negative.

However, the true lesson of any form of meditation is self-observation: learning to become the external observer of yourself.

Are you thinking too much? Did you end up in the middle of the storm? Stop. Breathe. Pay attention to the kind of thoughts you make when you fall into this vortex. You're just unnecessarily and fiercely slaughtering yourself, using weakening feelings such as guilt and shame.

Take a break, but a real one. From your work, from your children, from your usual life: the challenge is to change your habit. Sometimes it's enough to start with five minutes for yourself, some time for a coffee in an unknown place, a book to browse, a breath of fresh air from the window. These are all gestures which take on immense value, when done with awareness.

FEELING IN THE RIGHT PLACE

When you worry, you are basically hoping to control the flow of your life.

Eastern philosophies maintain that you have already chosen what will happen to you in life, even before your soul is incarnated, in order to have an experience which is useful for your growth. Therefore your conscious "I" must serenely accept every event, because it is not accidental, but previously established by you, for learning something during this incarnation.

From this point of view, you can easily understand that it is useless to try and change the course of things, because you would be putting yourself against universal laws: rather than wanting to solve what seems to be problems to you, you have to stop considering them as such and embrace them as "the most perfect thing for you right now".

Recognizing the time and the right place for everything happening to you is above all a form of liberation and peace: the belief that you are exactly where you should be, without worrying about the weight of justice or not of things, is a form of trust in life which is immediately returned with a profound release of all the emotion that holds you back in over-thinking.

Love every moment because it is exactly what you need!

CHOOSE WHAT TO CREATE

The law of attraction teaches that you create your reality by attracting it through thoughts. Technically this happens because similar ones attract each other, and you, surrounding yourself with a magnetic field impregnated by your negative thoughts, bring into your life just what you fear, because you think about it very often.

From this point of view, fear and concern are not defensive shields against your problems, but the best way to increase the likelihood of what happens to you.

Otherwise, having become aware of the power of your thoughts, you have to redirect the energy involved in the activity of thinking: transform that worm that oppresses you into something different, or let it go and turn your attention to something else, choosing to be happy.